for Peter
who published many of the poems
inside in TYR
with much love
Arvin   Allahabad Oct 98

The Transfiguring Places

The Transfiguring Places

poems by

Arvind Krishna Mehrotra

RAVI DAYAL Publisher
Delhi

Published by

RAVI DAYAL Publisher
51 E Sujan Singh Park
New Delhi 110003

Distributed by

ORIENT LONGMAN LTD
Bangalore   Bhubaneshwar   Calcutta   Chennai
Ernakulam   Guwahati   Hyderabad   Lucknow
Mumbai   New Delhi   Patna

ISBN 81 7530 019 1

Typeset by Rastrixi, New Delhi 110070
Printed at Pauls Press, New Delhi 110020

for my father
Deep Krishna Mehrotra
(1918 – 1979)

Contents

Acknowledgements

Acknowledgements are due to the editors of the following periodicals in which some of these poems first appeared: *Acumen, The Bombay Literary Review, Debonair, Encounter, The Gettysburg Review, Indian Review of Books, Literature Alive, London Magazine, Poetry Durham* and *Poetry Review*.

Approaching Fifty

Sometimes,
In unwiped bathroom mirrors,
He sees all three faces
Looking at him:

His own,
The grey-haired man's
Whose life policy has matured,
And the mocking youth's
Who paid the first premium.

Dry Farming

What do I measure, what do I sing?
　　Sing the heart's seizure, the fall
Of a king, so what if it's
　　Been sung before. So has the handicapped
Man waiting for traffic to thin, so has
　　The close at hand, the ode
To a safety pin. Or sing
　　The spread virus, the song everyone
Knows, ripped city buses and house full
　　Matinée shows. But if song
Dies in the tongue and all known methods
　　Fail, remember books, the other
Land, the double of the world
　　Outside, and to the terror
Of an unspoilt sheet
　　Bring the joy of *A Reader's Guide*.

Borges

Before the Ganges flows into the night,
   Before the knife rusts, the dream lose
Its crescent shape, before the tiger runs
   For cover in your pages, Borges, I must
Write the poem. Insomnia brings lucidity,
   And a borrowed voice sets the true one
Free: lead me who am no more than De Quincey's
   Malay, a speechless shadow in a world
Of sound, to the labyrinth of the earthly
   Library, perfect me in your work.

Inscription

Last night a line appeared,
Unbidden, unsigned;
It had eight memorable
Syllables. *I'll keep you,*

I said, falling asleep.
It's gone now,
And I write this to requite it,
And to mark its passage.

Memoranda

The milk's delivered at six o'clock.
Try nature cure for writer's block.

Travel north in a southbound train,
And cross the desert on the wheels of rain.

Unload the boats anchored in the bay.
Deepen the channel, dredge out the clay.

Once the hum stops there's nothing you can do.
Your best lines those that didn't come through.

Tongue-tied at times, at times colour-blind,
Go fishing, then. There's nothing wrong with your mind.

View the passing show with an inward eye.
The average man is only five feet high.

Art is long, who doesn't know that.
Keep pedalling, my friend, though the tyre's flat.

If not this, the next mile of verses
Could be the *annus mirabilis*.

At Seasons

In the close heat of summer
   An Iowa winter besets me —
An apartment in The Mayflower,
   My happy wife learning pottery.

In winter, the wet monsoon —
   Frog songs, low rumbling clouds,
Insects crawling on the arm,
   A heron shooting off its mouth.

On loony nights,
   Across the sealed window,
Hot winds chase
   Midwestern snow.

The Storm

There was little to tell it from
The other places we'd passed, Deoband,
Khatauli, the peasant towns of western
Uttar Pradesh. The June day was windless,
The sky a boiling white. The bus made
An unscheduled stop. A minor breakdown,
It seemed. The driver was talking
To a garage hand. Waiting for it to start,
We passed the time looking at the giant
Hoardings outside, the women
Standing with children at their hips
In littered doorways, the men sitting beside
Parked trucks, unshaven, drinking tea
— Their skins much lighter once.
A dog crossing the road halfway stopped
And, with head turned in the opposite direction,
Barked. Two blasts of the horn sounded,
And those who'd got down to stretch their legs
Hurried back. As the bus gathered speed,
I saw it quivering in the heat-haze,
A place whose name I hadn't known nor asked,
Which I sometimes think was Shiraz, or a firth
In the North Sea from where the skalds set out.
That night there was a storm, and the hail
Lay on the ground for weeks afterwards.

Ramapithecus and I

The young swamp he came to
Six million years ago,
His unfazed mother beside him,
His father recently dead,

Is the wallmap's mixed forest,
A dotted power line along its edge,
And the window's low, clouded hills,
Dolomite- and fossil-rich.

Making his home
Where his implements took him,
He waited for the rains to break.
Cutting my finger, it's his blood I taste.

Summer Notes

I

Mother in front, with shopping bag
    And umbrella; I in the middle;
Behind me a bespectacled
    Grandfatherly hodman carrying
A light load of bricks. The air
    Was clear as a bell that morning.
Back at my desk, night's events —
    Moon, jackfruit-tree, homing swallow —
Overtaking the window, hourglass sand
    The hour, I fell asleep. Our days
filled with insubstantial things,
    We dream to make up for lost time.

II

Evening, a book in my hand,
    Feet crossed on a plank of light
Slanting through the door,
    In the northern sky a cloud
About the size of Ireland looks down.

One by one lines darken
    On the unread page and early stars
Appear to take sides: going in,
    A phrase singing in my head,
A light rain of rhythms surrounds me.

III

Empty lorries pass us and a bored
   Holiday-maker waves from a bus.
Turning into a sidestreet we're enclosed
   In an ex-brigadier's garden
Where behind tall hedges and under
   A parrotless sky dwarf mango-trees
Carry on all fours full grown
   Fruit. Walking back past inconspicuous
Grocers' shops, our own lives
   Seeming blessed with retirement, a new
Bustle in the evening air: the sight
   Of common birds in exuberant flight.

IV

There's a world so they may seek advantage.
   Tumours, lyings-in, disorders of the skin,
Jobs and killings: the conversation
   Of the unfailably married gathered round
A tea wagon. A deaf-mute, a servant's daughter,
   Hops on the grass where a mongrel
Yawns; parked cars inch forward
   In receding light. 'How did the shaddock-tree die?'
I ask. A rockery where faded zinnias grow
   Forces its trunk and crumbly leaves
Hang at long intervals from
   Mortified branches; the ivy
That lashed it from base to crown sinking
   Petioles into the bark, rises in victorious tiers
On an adjoining wall. 'The last fruit
   Was its sweetest', someone says at the gate
As we leave our hosts, the hooded ivy, the poisoned
   Quarry, the animal kingdom of plants.

Old Survey Road

Where the land slopes
Toward the riverbed's
No man's land,
At the compound's edge,
Is a single tree,

Which is three trees
Grown from one sapling,
Or three saplings
Grown into one tree,
Mango, litchi, and peach

Ripening on its branches.
No botany textbook
Or illustrated dictionary
Gives its picture,
But in the record-breaking

Temperature of June,
The month of forest fires,
The green of parakeets
Flares in its foliage
And thieving children

Scrimmage in its shade,
To me their bruised knees
Recalling similar injuries,
Some yet to heal,
Others become rings.

The Inheritance

I

They were here
   Last night, outlaws,
Woodmen, visitors who came
   Nine years after
You died.

My mouth tasted
   Of sand. They
Sipped lemonade; stripped
   A family tree
Of foliage.

She took
   The silver, and he
The jade. I'll make,
   As I've this, a nest
In emptiness.

II

As others before you, you came here
   To die under trees
Which as a boy you'd climbed. Where

The litchi stood, east of the court,
   Is now a ditch, some
Kind man has covered with wild rose.

III

You left me sunset, the light
Of the polestar; to save me from summer
You left me the north, a strip of land
In that sad direction

To which I'm always returning. Among
Such articles I inherit, the gift
I brought you, a pair of socks, one size
Too big, for that is how fathers

Appear to sons, grown old themselves
In rented houses far from home.
I look at your hiding places again:
A shaving mirror; an aunt's profile.

IV

These rooms open
    Memory's stitches:
Your hand on my shoulder;
    The kiss on departure;
The letters, even the last,
    That gave nothing away.

Then the valley
    Seen from afar,
In a window's quiet,
    In a map on the wall,
Birds coming to
    Divided gardens.

The House

In the middle
Of a forest,
A house of stone.

Bats in the rafters,
Bat dung on the floor,
And hanging from a nail

A dentist's coat
Smelling pleasantly
Of chloroform.

Mud on his sandals
And smoke in his eyes,
On a railway platform

I saw him last,
Who passes before me
In the cheval-glass.

Locking Up

for I. Allan Sealy

Was that a barbet I heard
In the jujube tree?
Or walking sticks rattling
In an empty cupboard?
Are questions I ask
All summer long.
Then when vacation ends,
We pack our bags,
Lock up the place,
And return to the plains.

Not everything the ears hear
Can the tongue repeat: family lore,
The pied myna's call,
The blathering
Of a loose-tongued door,
The secrets that crawl
Out of dead servants' mouths.
My own snaps shut,
And I fall asleep listening
To the clickety-clack of the train.

It is taking me back
To the house I just locked.
It is winter.
I'm sitting in a wheelchair,
A rug wrapped around the knees,
Watching postmen go past the front gate
With nothing for me,
The afternoons
Getting longer each year,
And the light not dimming.

The Photograph
[New Delhi, 1958]

Amolak Ram Mehta and
Shanti Devi are flanked by
Their daughters and
A daughter-in-law;

Behind them,
In dark suits that'll
Never fade, the husbands
Stand shoulder to shoulder;

The grandchildren
Sit on the ground,
In front of their mothers.
At a distance of twenty feet,

Looking like a piece of ordnance,
Is the camera.
The photographer
Lowers the black cloth

And stepping forward, clicks.
Amolak Ram Mehta is dead,
So are the sons-in-law,
And his adoring children

Have carried the photograph
To Kalamazoo and Vancouver.
One's remained in my mother's house.
For years she's had it

On her bedroom wall
And never taken it down.
The spiders that live in it
Are of a golden colour.

16

The Fracture

Your mother is seventy.
One day she slips
And breaks her wrist.

You are not there
When this happens.
You are in Islington.

It's six weeks
Before you see her.
You take her to the doctor.

He asks her to open
And close her palm,
And she does as she is told.

He explains
Barton's fracture
To you

And holds an X-ray
Against the light.
You don't understand a thing

But nod all the same
And ask if they can replace
Hip joints in Dehra Dun.

I'm doing one this afternoon,
He says,
Filling another column

In her insurance form.
Your mother asks
If she should take more calcium.

My father, she says,
Sucked on bones
To make his own more strong

And lived to be ninety.
In two days
You have a train to catch

And are careful
About reaching her home
Safely.

Before leaving,
You advise her to be
More active

And to take long walks.

I Cannot Live Here All My Life

I cannot live here all my life.
The hour is set and streets explode.
A quiet man pulls out a knife.

They ride in peace who're born in strife,
The by-blows of a Tartar horde.
I cannot live here all my life.

Quick as death, the boys arrive.
Three go in, two watch the road.
A quiet man pulls out a knife.

It's like being buried alive.
Under the rubble lies one who said,
I cannot live here all my life.

As muscles waste and scars revive,
In the mind's pit left unexplored,
A quiet man pulls out a knife.

Eyewitnesses go blind, survive
The blown mouth. A mouth is closed.
I cannot live here all my life.
A quiet man pulls out a knife.

Scenes from a Revolving Chair

I

Day upon day, the outlook unchanged,
The long walk through elephant grass
In search of common speech. Sometimes
The nights are spent
In the middle of a borderless page,
And sometimes, unbroken clouds
Of late August darkening the frontier,
A wind rises in the octave branches.

II

The book lies open on two-voiced
Summer: the hawk-cuckoo's
Grey and white lines through hazeless
Air; overleaf, illuminated,
The copper-pod's long measures.
Standing like a bronze statue
In a public square, the city
Reads from the seasons.

III

After a heatwave and a night of storms
Have covered porcelain and rosewood
With a sheet woven with the threads
Of dust and rain,
A blue morning revives outside,
Offering to eyes what eyes cannot
Accept, unless a hand retouch
The unknowable picture.

IV

Without lifting their wings
The prey-birds climb
And fill the sky's dyed ground,
Throwing quilled shadows
Even as they move
Away from the eddying
River of consonants, the vowels that drown
Before leaden boats can reach them.

V

The moist-browed houses bury their dead
In unmarked valleys: the fanlight-eye
On which light does not fall,
The coping on which hard rain,
The bureau that will not be injured
By letters again. Steadily, for ever
Steadily, a sixty-year-old man
Blazes against a trembling wall.

Dream-figures in Sunlight

Why buy Bret Harte, I asked, when I was prepared to
supply home-grown fiction on the hoof?
                    Rudyard Kipling, *Something of Myself*

I wake up in the city where Kipling lived,
Fell in love and wrote plain tales,
Where Hsiuan-tsang in the seventh century
Saw mortal pilgrims making death-leaps

From an undying tree. The rampart stands,
The Ganges flows below, and nothing changes
In a hinterland whose dead-end streets
Have never known raiders. A hundred, a thousand

Years from now, may the sap-filled bough
Still print its shadow on running water,
And a dusty March wind blow its leaves
Towards a page of Kipling, a home-grown page.

Domicile

For the slashed cheek
And puckered knee
And unkept vow,

But as much for
The trips not made
To places of interest —

Like the Stone Age site
A busride away
In Mirzapur District —

Accept in recompense
This cone of light
In whose spell I sit,

A mechanical pencil
Gripped in my hand,
Like a microlith.

Last View from Church Lane

From rented rooms
The view of a tower
That broadcast rock pigeons
From the belfry when the hour

Struck, till one day
The irreparable chime-barrel
Clogged with droppings
And a wide crack appeared

Between minute and minute-hand.
We've changed too. My voice
Has grown blustery; yours
Is still as a moth's wings.

The Vase That Is Marriage

The vase is the painted figure
Of a vase, like a postcard-size print
Of, say, a still life with pawpaw.

The tablecloth is brown,
As in maps a mountain range is brown,
But the Java Sea is green, in which the vase,

Dragging its anchor, is a sailing junk.
The tablecloth is a hank of yarn,
Which doesn't make the vase potter's clay.

It never was that anyway.
When did he last, seeing the vase as a vase,
Put some flowers in, or not lack the desire?

To an Unborn Daughter

If writing a poem could bring you
Into existence, I'd write one now,
Filling the stanzas with more
Skin and tissue than a body needs,
Filling the lines with speech.
I'd even give you your mother's

Close-bitten nails and light-brown eyes,
For I think she had them. I saw her
Only once, through a train window,
In a yellow field. She was wearing
A pale-coloured dress. It was cold.
I think she wanted to say something.

Chekov Retold

No Yalta this, no lilac-hued sea,
Nor the time mid-autumn, but a district town
Of cobwebs and visitants, a night's journey

From the nearest coast. The March day
Unseasonably hot and the quarter hour,
By a one-armed clock, struck in a bee-hived tower.

From the west, a sirocco-like wind blowing,
Dragging a boy's kite, torn on one side,
To the meagre canopy of a myrobalan tree,

Buffalo cows mooing under it. Further
Up the road, in a margosa's leafless shade,
Unaware of the wide-eyed passers-by,

A man and a younger woman, his daughter's age,
Meet like thieves and a lap dog barks.
Where but in fiction are the lives they lead?

The Transfiguring Places

They teach you how to survive in the wild,
How stalk a quarry, which roots to eat,
Outdoor skills of no use in the street,
Where in sola hat of branching horns you chase

In grass and air the scent marks not there.
It's in the mind, the transfiguring,
Trysting places (banks, grocery stores) and
The trees you walk under, escaping,

Their leaves burning like light bulbs in the day
And a wind, long-toed, jostling you back
To the rear of a queue or the edge
Of a street, leaving you stamping the ground

With your feet and shaking your hatted head.
Wise up, I say, there's no running away
But taking the counterfoil or receipt
Crushed in your pocket in your composite stride.

The Reading Room

In a latitude where the nights
Are short and starless
Sitting on either side of a table
We expertly pitch our tent at end of day
Unable to see you in the failing light
I construct your mind from what you have to say

You tell me about a butterfly's wood-brown wings
The birdsong at five a.m.
That woke you like an alarm-clock
The desires of a mongrel bitch
Who litters in the cool of your verandah
A poem by Carlos Drummond which begins
'Carlos, keep calm, love / Is what you're seeing now'

You tell me about servants who are voyeurs
Fathers who are forgiving
Music masters and second lieutenants
You've driven crazy
An acquaintance who on second meeting
Confided her latest affair
You tell me about the wild times in Kalimpong

You tell me about hillsides and siblings
Pine cones and star signs
Law suits and pets
You tell me you're like a schoolgirl again
Discovering afresh in a candy-striped dress
The cloven leaf and the parts of a flower
You tell me how clever you are

As the kettle hisses
And you keep talking
My stretched hand touching
The raised lines of your skin
I want to tell you it's nothing you say
But the singing voice you say it in

Tailorbird

Bring it to me, I'll
   Turn your life,
The tailorbird said.
   I was listening.

Reading the sports page
   One Thursday morning,
I saw her darting out
   Of a flowering tree.

Heading the wrong way,
   She kept coming
Towards me, stolen thread
   Held in her beak,

To tack on my jacket
   A tailorbird's wings.
(I found you in the dust,
   She would say.)

The door still ajar,
   And she calling out,
The terrazzo floor
   Dropping below me,

I sailed in fields
   Where gale-winds blew
But each leaf
   Was still, as if

On a windless day.
    Then evening fell,
The living room's
    Colours changed,

The gates
    Of the mausoleum
Closed for the night,
    And small birds

With their love-cries
    Filled a flowering tree.
Looking up
    From the sports page

I heard
    A tailorbird say,
Bring it to me, I'll
    Turn your life.

Nautical, 1

Those jetty lights are wax candles
   Flickering over bald cabbages.
At makeshift stalls behind
   The Accountant General's office,
Gray-stubbled, fecund, homebound clerks —
   Their lastborn the same age
As their first grandchild —
   Haggle for perishables.
Their frenzied voices roll and heave
   As she comes into view, vanishes,
Reappears, weighed down by stout canvas
   Shopping bags, and squeezing
The car keys in her hand.
   She comes alongside,
And for what seems a long time,
   Out of the corner of her eye
Witches me watching her buy
   Cucumbers and spring onions.

Nautical, 2

Early travellers to upland towns
   And the Coromandel coast, whose feet
Trod the ground but walked on the sea,
   Have left accounts of mermaid sightings.

I sighted one as I ran across a street
   On an errand. The traffic light was green
And cars, their headlamps dipped, braked or swerved.
   I bought a loaf and took the same route home.

The return felt shorter, the luminous ports
   Touched in reverse order. The sky was black,
As before a storm, when I drew ashore,
   Scaly thighed and with weed-hung arms.

From a Neoteric Codex

Better, by far, the black economy
Of night. By the stars short changed,
To have leapt over a magistrate's gate
At dawn and shoeless fled across
The dung-pits of Rome, than stood
Twitchingly at noon in comical
Disguise and as the cuckoo-clocks chimed
At one blow passed from stunned old age
To erect youth and back, only worse,
The insides upside down and hanging out.
Fish, coming up to the aquarium wall,
Glued their noses to it and watched,
As they did on the day, since erased, when,
A Hamadryad in spring, recumbent
On a couch, you said *Give me poison*.
I wish I had. And yet you won't
Walk out of history just like that,
Unidentified, uncelebrated, and unspat
(One cuts one's losses the best one can),
No Catullus to your Lesbia though I am.

Cedars

In the mountains
No disguise helps.
No beret, camouflage jacket,
And wire-rimmed specs,
No checking into hotels
Under a false name even.

The road narrows,
Becomes steep;
You go past the clocktower,
The silversmiths' shops,
And two cows grazing,
And come upon snow peaks
Glittering like trophies
In the sun.

Nothing prepares you for that,
Nor for the hill woman
You stop on the way
To ask about the trees.
She has thick ankles
And a slow walk,
And says they're cedars.

Trouvaille

Too numerous to be hidden safely in books,
The letters keep falling out, the early ones
Unsigned, the latest full of old accusations.
Picking one up I read along the fold,
What makes you say all this is make-believe?

Your round, legible hand, mainly, but also
The earth's shape, the exactness of distances,
The coldness of ice, the happiness of others,
The eight parts of the day, the sight of hills.
Things must remain as they are, and I am changed.

Beggarhood

Loping along back roads,
Or sitting in his verandah
In a deckchair,
Or waiting outside phone booths,
Invisible to none
But himself, he's
The man with 6/6 vision.

It is November
And he sees March,
The jacaranda putting forth
An affluence of mauve blossoms.
To see it in November, though,
Is the bronze coin he seeks —
Small, countable, and legal tender.

The Cartographer

He would draw
Anything once:
Peninsulas;
Archipelagoes;
Grassless, unsettled,
Jagged-edged islands;
Landlocked countries
Of cold latitudes,
Exposed like bricks
When empires fell.
Times and places
Close to the self-applauding heart.

Not any more.
Now he draws less,
And such features only
As memory in receding shows:
Pit-heads
And coal-veins;
Tributaries that fall short of rivers
That fall short of the sea;
The dots of broken
Cease-fire lines;
The yellow or red
Of internal boundaries.